What I Eat

Healthy Living

We can stay healthy.

We can eat good food,
to stay healthy.

Look at me.

I am eating fruit.

Fruit is good to eat.

Look at me.

I am eating yoghurt.

Yoghurt is good to eat.

My sandwich

is good to eat.

My sandwich

has meat and cheese

and tomato.

11

Ice-cream

is good to eat, too!

Ice-cream is a treat.

We all eat good food!

15

Do you eat good food?

16